T0208442

A Gumbo
of
Poems & Quotes

A Gumbo of Poems & Quotes

Aurora L. Threats

Library of Congress Control Number: 2020905168
ISBN: Hardcover   978-1-7960-9270-7
                 Softcover   978-1-7960-9271-4
                 eBook   978-1-7960-9272-1

Print information available on the last page.

Rev. date: 07/18/2023

To order additional copies of this book, contact:
Xlibris
844-714-8691
www.Xlibris.com
Orders@Xlibris.com
810777

CONTENTS

This book is dedicated to the memory of my brother

Chief Aaron "Rudy" Threats

A compassionate pillar in the community. With nearly four decades of remarkable service in law enforcement, your commitment went above and beyond, selflessly serving others. Through your creation of movie nights, you brought entertainment, enjoyment, and unity to families and churches, leaving a lasting impact.

This book stands as a tribute to your unwavering strength, resilience, and unwavering faith, forever preserving your remarkable legacy.

Acknowledgments

First and foremost, I humbly give thanks to God, the author, and finisher of my faith. His loving guidance has been with me every step of my life and this journey.

To my beloved son Fred L. Threats, Sr., my wonderful mother Ethel M. Threats, my dear family, and friends, words cannot adequately express the depth of my love and appreciation for you. As you journey through the pages of this book, it is my sincerest hope that its contents will resonate within you, warming your hearts in the same way that your love and presence have filled mine. I am truly grateful for being blessed with your constant source of love, inspiration, and unwavering encouragement.

To all my awesome followers on social media, I extend my heartfelt thanks for your engagement and invaluable support. The love, likes, shares, and comments you have generously bestowed upon me have touched my heart deeply. I am truly grateful for the connection we have forged. Your continuous support means the world to me.

Lastly, I want to express my sincere gratitude to Sherilyn Powell for her exceptional photography. Through her skill and dedication, she has beautifully enhanced the pages of this book, adding a visual dimension that complements the essence of the poems and quotes. Sherilyn, thank you for your stunning photography, which has made this book even more special.

I hope "A Gumbo of Poems & Quotes" becomes a treasured part of your collection and brings you as much joy and inspiration as it has brought to me.

A Hug

When life becomes a battle
And nothing seems to matter
Confusion inside the mind
Peace within, I cannot find
A hug is all I need
All I need is a hug
My spirit is drifting and broken
No words that are spoken
Seem to keep my mind sane
When my heart is in pain
All I need is a hug
A hug is all I need
A hug, a hug, indeed

"Love is a hug that forever remains in your heart."

A Portrait Of Friendship

In the park where nature's beauty gleams
We embark on a bike ride along the bayou streams
A portrait of friendship, a brushstroke so perfect
Where pleasure and laughter reflect without defect

Like an art gallery exhibit with colors so grand
We pedal through the park, side by side
Lush greenery surrounds us, a picturesque sight
As we journey together, basking in nature's light

Amidst this paradise, Southern Magnolia trees
Beautifully swaying in the breeze
Their ivory blossoms, fragrant and pure
Symbolize our friendship, timeless and sure

The bayou's gentle waters flow by our side
Reflecting the sky's hues with a shimmering tide
Trees sway in harmony, their branches reaching high
Providing shade and comfort under the sunlit sky

With every pedal, we feel the wind's gentle caress
Whispering secrets of serenity and happiness
The fragrance of wildflowers fills the air
Enhancing the beauty, and the fun we share

In this idyllic park, an overture of sounds
Birds singing songs, nature's music abounds
The laughter of children leaves rustling with ease
A serenade, of melodies that appease

Through ups and downs, our path may twist and turn
But our friendship remains strong, as we learn
Together we navigate life's winding trails
Sharing joys and sorrows, our spirits always prevail

In this botanical paradise, a happy place
A treasure of love, a smile on our face
With every stroke of the pedal, memories we create
A sweet connection like a bowl of cherries, truly great

So let us cherish this portrait, painted with care
A masterpiece of friendship, we will forever share
In this park, where nature's beauty gleams
Our bond grows stronger, and so do our dreams

"With a true friend, your secrets are held securely,
and don't take wings and fly in the wind."

Supercilious

Sometimes my eyes would fill with tears
From their supercilious sneers
As I walked down the lonely streets
I realized the world, the world was at my feet

As the story goes according to them

I wasn't going to amount to anything
I wasn't going to succeed
Because my mother was single
With a born out-of-wedlock kid

With their heads held so high
Their eyes reached up to the sky
They felt they were on the ball
Pretending they had it all

They whispered, who does she think she is?
Look at her she's in everything
Everything like what?
Everything that they felt I shouldn't be in

Like my aspirations, and ol' gosh my individuality
They didn't look around to see that this girl
Was extraordinary - - She was destined to succeed
Clearly, they were out of touch with reality

Thinking they were better than most
Living in a make-believe world
With no real vision of their own
And, considered mine to be lost

They said I wasn't going to amount to anything
And, going to college I would be back
Yeah, I did come back, but with an education in my sack
And, found them criticizing and stabbing each other in the back

I not only succeeded I crushed your supercilious stance
Reducing it to dust, leaving no room for a second chance
I shattered your illusions, shattered your beliefs
Proving that greatness can emerge from beneath

You know talkin' loud and saying nothing
Was supposed to be better than my blessed
Ugh pardon, the interruption
That's why you end up with less

Take heed, my dear friends
Pride comes before destruction
And an arrogant spirit before a fall
Now, that's real y'all

See, my single mother, taught me to have faith
She taught me the importance of education
She gave it to me straight
To step up to the plate and pull my weight

Put down, after -put down, after -put down
Passed over, doubted, and dismissed
Please forgive me

But while you were blowing insults and
Supercilious words in the wind
That was supposed to diminish my being
God was blessing, designing, and guiding me to my destiny

"Nothing scares a hater more than your success."

The Clock Keeps Ticking

Time doesn't sit still
There is a greater purpose
The clock keeps ticking

Life is but a fleeting beat

The world spins fast, the clock ticks on
Before you know it a day is gone
Time waits for no one, gone, gone, gone

Seize the day, the hour, the moment
And make the most of every component
For dreams don't come true on their own

You have to keep pushing

Don't wait for the stars to align
Or for the perfect plan to design
Take the first step, a leap of faith

And let your heart guide you to your place

Greater awaits don't drag your feet
Dance, run, and skip to the beat
Live your life with passion and zeal

Cherish each moment it's precious
And, so are the days of our life
Time lost can never be recaptured

It's gone, gone, gone

"Jealousy is a sneaky little creature that tries to hide, but its true colors always shine through in the way you speak, your actions, your attitude, and in your body language."

Honey Shine

Don't be shy, don't hide away
Let your light shine, each and every day
For within your light lies great power

You hold within, a spark of divine
A flame that burns, a glow that shines
A gift unique, that's hard to find

Honey shine your light splendidly

There lies a beauty that comes from within
A glow that gives others a sense of delight
Dear one, your beacon is so bright

So go ahead, light up the way,
With love and joy, every single day
Don't ever shrink or downplay

You're a gem, a flower, a work of art

Your compassion for others is heavenly
Your beauty is like a melody
Let your light shine with all your might

Be fearless, be brave, be bold
For you are meant to make a mark
For in your light, the world will see

The brilliance of your destiny

"Don't let anything or anybody stand in between you and God."

Jesus, You're All I Need

You're here inside each breath
You guide me to forgive and forget
Within every heartbeat, I find in You
Strength and grace to face all that I go through

In You alone, I find my purpose
In You alone, I find my joy
You're the one who knows me best
My thoughts, my fears, my distress

May my life be a reflection of you
May others see you shining through
Your love is greater than all
You answer when Your name I call

You're the blazing fire within my soul
Igniting passions, making me feel whole
May my life echo Your love and grace
A testament to Your redeeming embrace

My rock, my refuge, the fire in my heart
In You alone, my desires find their start
May my life forever shine and reflect
The love and grace that You perfect

Jesus, my all in all, my Saviour and friend
In You, my joy knows no bounds, no end
With every beat of my heart, I'll proclaim
Your love, Your name forever I acclaim

"Never trust someone you don't trust."

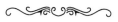

Had It Not Been For

Where, oh where would we be

Had it not been for those who came before
Pioneers who opened wide the door
The way forward may have been unclear
But their legacy still echoes, loud and clear

Charles Drew with his blood bank innovation
George Washington Carver's agricultural creation
Benjamin Banneker's mathematical skill
Frederick Douglas's voice, speaking with will
Booker T. Washington's dedication to education
A generation uplifted, through his determination

Where, where would we be?

Their faith was their compass leading the way
Courage was a song that rang out strong
From weary tears, they found the strength to rise
And faced fear head-on, with unblinking eyes

Oh, had it not been for the inspiring and strong

Harriet Tubman leading the Underground Railroad
Sojourner Truth powerful words that flowed
Madam CJ Walker triumphs as a self-made millionaire
Mary McLeod Bethune education her wings
Rosa Parks refused to give up her seat
Their legacy lives on, their bravery hard to beat

The prayers of the upright, so pure and true
Guided them toward what they must do
Believing in better, they took up the task
And shared with all their mission to unmask

Where, where would we be?

Had it not been for your light in the dark
W.E.B. Du Bois igniting a powerful spark
Thurgood Marshall fighting for justice's mark
Malcolm X challenged societal stark

Medgar Evers unwavering in the face of fear
Dr. Martin Luther King Jr's dream was crystal clear
Robert and John F. Kennedy's, voices sincere
Oh, tell me where would we be without you near

Where, oh where would we be?

For it is because of their resplendent hue
That we can be everything, anything true
A testament to their enduring might
Their legacy, forever shining bright

If it had not been for the Lord's divine decree
Paths made straight and clear
Jackie Robinson's light, Major League's pioneer
Jessie Owen's sprint, unmatched, swift, and fleet
Joe Louis, champion, fist solid as concrete
Eddie G. Robinson, gridiron unscored an unbeaten roar
Their legacies shine, and blessed blessings pour

Let us honor the legacy of those who led
Their vision, their passion forever widespread
May we carry their torch with unwavering grace
And build a better world, for every human race

"Greatness is not just a dream, but a destiny we pursue."

Grandma's Kitchen

In Grandma's kitchen love was the key
Where magic unfolds, filling hearts with glee
From the crackling stove to the worn-out spoon
A medley of flavors, the sweetest tune

Handwritten recipes, with stories to tell
Through generations, they lovingly dwell
From gumbo that warms in winter's chill
To etouffee that ignites a fiery thrill

From red beans and rice, a nourishing delight
To jambalaya, vibrant and bright
The tantalizing rhapsody reaches its peak
As flavors dance upon the palate, unique

Around the table, laughter and stories abound
As we settled in, our voices a joyful sound
Grandma's kitchen transformed, into a sacred space
Where love and togetherness found their place

In the oven's embrace, a sweet dedication
We whisk the ingredients, both old and new
Blending traditions and dreams that ensue
With spices of courage and flavors of grace

In Grandma's kitchen, memories were made
With homemade treats, love could never fade
Banana pudding, and peach cobbler taste so
Good they'll make you shout
A testament to Grandma's love and culinary glory

In Grandma's kitchen, traditions abide
As we gather 'round, side by side
The legacy lives on, forever unbroken
In the love and flavors, forever awoken

Sunday's after church, a tradition held dear
Gather at Grandma's with love and cheer
For it was more than just a meal we'd share
It was a bond, a memory, a moment rare

From the kitchen to the table heavenly divine
A sacred and intimate space to dine
In each dish prepared, memories loom
In Grandma's kitchen, love finds its room

"Every bit of sweetness makes every moment all the more scrumptious."

Whispers of Purpose

In a world filled with chaos and noise
Listen closely to the silent voice
In the whispers of purpose, a subtle call
A guiding voice that echoes through it all

Whispers of purpose, gentle and wise
Echoing in the depths where passion lies
Listen closely to the secrets it imparts
Revealing the path that aligns with your heart

Sweeten your own ambition, set yourself free
Create a melody that's uniquely thee
Cling to the calling deep within
Unveil the treasures you hold therein

With a skip in your step and a smile so wide
Let the whispers of purpose be your guide
Kick up your heels, in a joyful display
As you take heart, along life's highway

In each whisper, a message hidden deep
A secret language only our hearts can keep
The whispers guide us, like a sacred thread
Leading us closer to the path we're meant to tread

In the grandeur of life, take your place
With courage and dignity, just in case
Let not the doubts or fears impede
For you're the architect of your own creed

So let us listen, with attentive ears
To whispers soft, where purpose does appear
For they shall lead us, with their gentle plea
To fulfill the destiny that's meant to be.

"True confidence doesn't compete it shines."

The Good Life

The good life is a state of mind
A gratitude for what we have
A recognition, of life's blessings
A celebration of the present

The good life is a choice we make
To appreciate the beauty that exists
To savor the little things
To find joy in everyday

In moments that are fleeting
In the warmth of a smile
In the embrace of a loved one
In the laughter that fills the air

It's not defined by wealth or fame
But by the contentment, we feel inside
By the peace that resides in our hearts
By the love that surrounds us

It's in the sunsets that paint the sky
In the gentle breeze that whispers through the trees
In the taste of a delicious meal
In the music that moves our souls

So let us cherish each precious moment
And live the good life big or small
For it's in the simple pleasures
That we find the greatest happiness of all

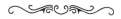

"If you keep negativity at bay happiness will blossom as the good life unfold."

Enchanting Blooms

Upon the shores of tranquil dreams, I tread
Where fragrant petals caress the gentle air
In Bora Bora's embrace, my heart is fed
By a symphony of peace, a moment rare

Turquoise lagoon, a mirror calm and clear
Reflects the sky, a canvas vast and bright
With pristine sands that whisper, "Come near
Find solace here, in nature's purest light"

In my flower garden's serene embrace
A haven of scents that soothe weary minds
Each blossom a moment of tranquil grace
Where love, peace, and dreams align

The Eiffel Tower stands, majestically, in the distance
Symbolic of dreams that reach the lofty sky
Yet in my garden's blooms, love finds its instance
Its beauty reveals more than meets the eye

In every corner, colors softly blend
Like whispers carried by a gentle breeze
Their fragrant petals, a soothing blend
Creating serenity that puts my soul at ease

Let us cherish the wonders of life, day by day
Hold dear the beauty woven in each bloom
In solitude, our souls find a peaceful way
Amidst the garden's enchantment, its sweet perfumes

As I wander through this cherished sanctuary
With Bora Bora's essence within my soul
In each blooming wonder, the solace I carry
A garden's serenity that makes me whole

With gratitude, I treasure life's gentle song
In my flower garden, emotions freely flow
Where nature's beauty and scents belong
And peaceful memories forever grow

May my cherished garden forever bloom
Infusing my world with serenity true
In whispered breezes, love finds its room
A sanctuary where dreams come into view

"The enchanting beauty of flowers carries secrets, and brings joy to the soul, much like a bird's sweet song."

Let Go

Let go of comparing
It leads to jealousy

Let go of jealousy
It leads to anger

Let go of anger
It leads to blame

Let go of blame
It leads to lying

Let go of lying
It leads to gossiping

Let go of gossiping
It leads to disappointment

Let go of disappointment
It leads to stress

Let go of stress
It depresses, oppresses, suppresses
And leads to no progress
By which no one is impressed

Let go; it leads to forgiveness
Realize
You
Are
Blessed

"Sometimes telling a person when they're wrong
is what they need to get it right."

It's in the Pudding

If you've never been told
It's time for you to know
No matter how hard it seems
Keep reaching for your dream

(Wisdom)
Listening to a pinch of wisdom
Is how so many have risen
Listening to something old, something new
Something you already knew

(Passion)
Inside you, there is a voice
Inside that voice is your soul
Inside your soul is your passion
Inside your passion is all you can imagine

(Believe)
Feel your power
Feel your power
With all your mind, heart, and soul
Believe it, dream it, be it

(Faith)
Faith it until you make it
Faith the size of a mustard seed
Is all you need to succeed
Faith that if life gives you lemons
Take it and make lemonade

(Courage)
Having just an ounce of courage
Will surround you like a shield
From the rain, the lightning, and
The thunder of a grumbling storm

It's in the puddin'
That if you delight yourself in the power
And add the right ingredients
To love and self-love
You can conquer the world

"Life has taught me that what you allow will continue."

Imagine

Imagine there's no sun
That beautiful blush of light
To rise upon the horizon
Into the promise of day

Imagine
The petals unfold
When the gleaming rays of day
Warmly kiss the world

Did you ever stop to think
The sun that shines on you and me
The star that lights the world
Is our life and breath?

Imagine there's no sun
To give a smile to the world
That can blossom and grow
Then feed our starving souls

Imagine
That satin sheen of daylight
Such a splendor to all creation
Is our flame of life

Did you ever stop to think
The sun that shines on you and me
The star that lights the world
Is our life and breath?

Imagine there's no sun
To dry the tears of rain
To melt the cold away
To shimmer the morning dew like diamonds

Imagine
The grass silently grows
And life becomes sweeter
When that ever-so-wonderful ball of light
Pours its flaming love upon the earth

Did you ever stop to think
The sun that shines on you and me
The star that lights the world
Is our life and breath?

"Many have lost sight of who they are trying to live
a life not assigned to them."

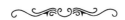

Ditch Digging

Digging ditches all 'round town
Trying to drag others down
You slander their name
Then laugh out loud

It's so funny it's a flash
In the middle of a crowd
Hoping it will bring hurt and shame
And they will do the same

Here's what will happen

You won't hear the whisper
Of the oncoming twister
You won't see the rain
That will numb you with pain

Careful with the plots, the snares
And setting booby traps
The one you set for him or her
May be for you perhaps

What you meant for evil
Will deliver them from atrocity
Will turn out good for them
And leave you with animosity

The ditch you dig will flood
Flood you with misery

Burden you with guilt
No sleep for the weary
Truly, truly, you will weep
With no peace in the deep

"Kindness is a sweet taste to the soul."

A Message in a Bottle

Upon distant shores, an alluring smile of grace
In a letter, love finds its rightful place
A wanderer unable to sail the mystic sea
But a message in a bottle carries love's plea

From dawn's gentle mist to evening's cascading sunset
Across uncharted waters, to somewhere thereon
May it find its way into your loving arms
A message in a bottle, bound by tender charms

May a solitary traveler's wish be heard
No longer adrift, a heart deeply stirred
May this message, in a big way
Bring beauty and solace to you all your days

With smiles collected, treasured, and saved
Enclosed in a bottle, love's treasure engraved
Upon the dreamy sea, it set sail
Through waters clear as diamonds, gleaming and mild

One day it shall find you, dear friend of mine
As the sea's gentle kiss caresses the shore
The tides will dance and wave, joyful and clear
Bound together by currents, always forever

But as a new day dawns, the dream departs
Yet hope remains, its radiant glow imparts
For love's message in a bottle forever gleams
A testament of love that transcends all hearts

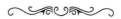

"Sprinkling kindness is like spreading magic and joy all around."

For Such A Time As This

As the world seemed to tremble and shake
We didn't know how much we could take
We avoided gatherings and closed our doors
And prayed for a better tomorrow

For such a time as this

Oh-oh the darkness seemed so deep
Heavily burdened many could not sleep
One thing is for sure a paradigm shift
The whole world needed a lift

From cities to boroughs, to towns
Anxiety was high and even fear
With most of the world shut down
We still pushed and persevered

The pandemic made us realize
Just how much we'd taken for grant - even life
Our freedom to move and be
Now a precious gift we see

Somehow we found the courage to keep going
To face each day and be reborn
To navigate the chaos with steadfast love
By a light that cascaded from above

We unveiled the strength we possess
The power of humanity, in times of distress
The grace of God brought us through
For such a time as this

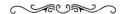

"In moments of uncertainty, find your cozy space, embrace love, and worries unfriend".

Secret Prayer

Worrying from morning to evening
And evening to morning
Go into your closet
Take it to God in secret prayer

In secret where none other
Can hear you, none other
Can see you, none other
Can take what's yours and utter

Go into your room
Close your door
With God and self, be honest
Secret things belong to him

Go to him in secret prayer
Secret prayer holds many treasures
It holds the key to your dreams

He will reveal things
Things that your eyes have not seen
Your ears have never heard
Things that have never entered your heart
Things that have been prepared for you

If you ask, he will come through
Reward you openly out of the blue
No one can take it, shake it, undo it
Throw a stone, and break it

If you let the words of your mouth
And the meditation of your heart
Be acceptable in thy sight
He will take you from here to there

Because of your faith in Jesus
He will leave everyone speechless

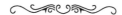

"Life has taught me that we create our own strengths and weaknesses
through the thoughts we think and the words we speak."

Level Up

She used to hide in the shadows
Afraid to stand out from the crowd
But something inside her was stirring
A voice that cried out loud

It said, "You are capable of greatness
You are strong and you are bold
Don't let your fears and doubts hold you back
It's time to break the mold"

So she took a deep breath and stepped forward
With dignity into the light of the day
And faced her fears head-on
She felt her strength and became bold

Her ambitions were no longer on hold
Now she's a girl who's unstoppable
She leveled up and she's phenomenal
Her confidence is a mystery that's unsolvable

She found herself and claimed her space
She leveled up with grace
And showing the world her full potential
Her beauty, her worth, her strength

She's done with playing small
With shrinking and hiding in the crowd
She's ready for the world y'all
And she's answering her call

When you feel the urge to level up
Click your heels three times and smile
For you are capable of greatness
And, able to go the extra mile

So watch out world here she comes
This girl is on the rise
She's leveling up and reaching for the skys
With determination in her eyes

"If you don't get some motivation, you may get eliminated."

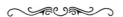

The Strong & Resilient

The strong and resilient will rise
Beaming with determination in their eyes
They rise with courage, embracing the unknown
The power of endurance is sown

The world may try to cast its doubt
To erase their dreams with a scornful hand
But they stand tall, unwavering throughout
For they possess what no one can command

Within their hearts, a fire fiercely gleams
Nurtured by purpose, a sight that redeems
Aware of their worth, a resounding sound
With every stumble, rebirth is found

No force can steal what's meant to be
No hand can snatch predestination
On wings like eagles, they will soar
A truth that none can ever ignore

Through trials, they discover their might
And become light in the darkest night
They gather fragments, piece by piece
To forge a strength that won't decrease

In the face of adversity's frown
They turn the world upside down
And in the twinkling of an eye
With newfound wings, they learn to fly

For God's plan lies within their core
A sacred flame forevermore
No one can take what's truly theirs
No one can erase the answered prayers

So let them stumble, let them fall
They'll rise again, defying it all
Their spirit is unbreakable, forever strong
Proving doubters wrong, against the throng

In the face of storms, they'll find their way
Guided by faith, they'll never sway
For they know deep in their soul
God's love will always make them whole

No matter what life may put in their path
They'll rise, unyielding, and embrace the aftermath
For in their hearts, they hold the key
To unlock the strength that set them free

"I believe in the power of *me* that comes directly from God
and no other source outside of him."

You Surpass Them All

In truth, it is inscribed
A living testament, deeply imbued
That many women do noble things
But you surpass them all

Through storms and shadows, you prevail
Your spirit fierce, like a mighty gale
Your enigma captivates, seekers who pursue
Yearning to grasp your serene soul's view

No need to prove, to disavow
For who you are, none can endow
A heart, a treasure trove of love
Guided by virtues from high above

Above the noise, where greatness sworn
Some are drawn away, some are drawn toward
With hands that toil, you build your own emprise
So let the world witness your extraordinary rise

A force that surges, fierce and true
A capacity to conquer, to break through
You surpass them all, it's undeniably true
A woman of courage, strong and true

Oh, dear sister, continue to blaze
A masterpiece of strength, a vibrant maze
In every stride, you redefine
The essence of greatness, uniquely thine

No earthly measure can truly capture
The depth of your spirit dreams that fracture
For you are more than words can convey
A masterpiece of tensility in every way

Sister, your presence, is a testament true
To the unlimited strength that lies within you
May your path be blessed, your spirit free
Forever brilliant, for all to see

Let this praise echo, your greatness recall
For you, dear sister, surpass them all
You touch and inspire many hearts deeply
A gift that beams uniquely

So let them marvel, in awe and wonder
As you blaze trails, like rolling thunder
For in your being, truth is found
A queen of hearts, forever crowned

"With hands that toil build your own emprise."

Notes of Inspiration

(Verse 1)
On this journey of life, we search for what feels true
Like a Master Chef, we stir, we stew
A medley of poems and quotes, like ingredients in a pot
Creating a gumbo of inspiration that hits the perfect spot

(Pre-Chorus)
Take your time let the rhythm guide
Like a Master Chef, we won't hide
From the flavors, we create to the love we ignite
We'll cook up a medley that simmered just right

(Chorus)
Take your time, let the music take flight
With verses that heal and quotes that inspire
We'll create a menu that takes us higher

(Verse 2)
In this kitchen of words, we blend wisdom and grace
Like a Master Chef, leaving a lasting trace
Every line carefully crafted with passion and care
We'll serve up a feast of positivity we all can share

(Bridge)
We mix the flavors of love and reflection
Crafting verses that evoke connection
Every thought, every line, a delightful surprise
A song that warms hearts and opens eyes

(Pre-Chorus)
Take your time, let the words simmer and ignite
Just like a Master Chef, everything measured just right
With rhythm and rhyme, a delectable cuisine
Crafting a medley that makes our spirits gleam

(Chorus)
Take your time, let the music take flight
With verses that heal and quotes that inspire
We'll create a menu that takes us higher

(Outro)
So let the music play, let it fill the air
Our creation, a reminder to care
With each line and quote, we'll spread love and hope
Like a Master Chef, crafting a piece that helps us cope

"Always serve up a feast - a party of smiles and delicious positivity."

 Practice What You Preach

In a village not too far, full of wisdom and speech
There lived a preacher, with a lesson to teach
He preached to his flock, with zeal and might
"Practice what you preach!" was his guiding light

But this preacher, you see, had a little quirk
He preached about patience, but would often irk
For he'd tap his foot, and check his watch
Impatience was his weakness, oh what a botch

He spoke of forgiveness, with a righteous tone
Yet held grudges galore, to his very own bone
He'd frown at his neighbor, with an accusing stare
"Practice what you preach!" they'd exclaim, beware

He preached of honesty, and truthfulness too
But little white lies, oh, he'd easily spew
His congregation was puzzled, scratching their heads
"Practice what you preach!" they whispered in threads

He'd speak of compassion, for every living soul
But scold dogs, as they played with a joyful roll
All the folks were baffled, what a curious man
"Practice what you preach!" they yelled, as loud as they can

One shiny Sunday morning, the preacher took heed
To the whispers and cries, his congregation's need
He stood at the pulpit, with a heavy heart
And vowed to change, to make a fresh start

From that day on, he practiced what he taught
No longer did he falter or come to a halt
With patience, he listened and forgave with grace
His honesty shone, a smile on his face

Compassion he showered, on each living thing
From stray dogs to birds, he made their hearts sing
All the folks rejoiced, the change was a sight
"Practice what you preach!" they laughed with delight

So remember this as you journey along
For life is a mirror, reflecting what we do
For life is a stage, where humor does beseech
"Practice what you preach!" or change your speech

"Since practice makes perfect, practice doing good, and good will follow you."

Listen

Give ears to the wind softly rustling the waters
And sighing as it breeze through the trees
Whispering, "You are more than you see"
Encouraging you to live your dreams

Put God first, and you will never be last
Don't allow your future to be dictated by your past
Decide not to be led by what others say and do
And learn to be, to yourself, true

The trees will all clap their hands
The hills will sing you a song
God will prosper you as planned
Sometimes you have to get in your zone
And do you alone

When others are without a passion
They may not get the picture
As offbeat as it seems
They may not understand what it
Feels like to go after a dream

"Your playbook is your secret weapon it's the
key to your dreams and aspirations."

Pearls of Wisdom

Dignity, you might think it's old-fashioned
But some things never go out of style
Presence is a fashion statement
It's sweet; it's fragrant

It's the fragrance of the soul
It's tame, as gentle as a lamb
Let beautiful pearls of wisdom
Flow from your lips

You can be insulted, cut down with words
Ssssh, don't speak; use your enigma
You may be a million miles from reality
But don't compromise your dignity

It's decency, honesty, wit, and power
It's soft and takes the sting out of loud
It's the highest form of self-respect
Anyone secure can project

Always remember the principle of love
Do to others as you would have them do to you
Even if you should slip and stumble
Don't lose your rhythm

Oh my goodness
Hush your mouth
Excuse me
Thank you
Bless your heart

Yesterday, today, tomorrow, still the same
Let goodness within your heart
Be a lasting beauty, gentle and tranquil spirit
Precious words of wisdom to all who listen

"Wisdom, understanding, and common sense come from God."

Flattering Lips

Let's talk betrayal
Y'all ready?

Those same flattering lips
That kissed you on the cheek
Like the morning pearly light
Are the same lips that will cut you
Like a diamond cutting glass
Those same lips that asked you to help them please
Are the same lips that turn so cold
You'd think it's a hard winter freeze
Those same lips that smiled at you
Like a sunflower reaching for the sun
Are the same lips that will whisper like the wind
Those same lips that gossip to you
Like a song a thrush bird
Will sing from the highest branches of a tree
To put your business in the streets
Those same beautiful lips you thought were so cool
May have a double heart that's bitter and cruel
Those same flattering lips
That speak so sweet
Will create a buzz
Like a bee with honey in its mouth
And a sting in its tail
Those flattering lips
Are the same lips
That denigrate, vilify
Backhand compliment, ridicule, criticize
Roast, toast, undermine, blindside, snag, tag

Then try to play you for a fool
Until one day, they become your footstool
Because they forgot the golden rule
Do unto others as you would have them
Do unto you

"Everybody who laughs and talks with you ain't for you."

You Are Good

If you do good
You are good
If you believe in good
You are good
If you reason good
You are good
If you speak good
You are good
If you render to good
You are good
If you eat good
You are good
If you feel good
You are good
If you don't withhold good
You are good
If you cherish good
You are good
If you are good with good
Good will be good by you
It will follow you
If it follows you
You are good

"True confidence whispers softly."

Girl Power

We dress with love, embracing who we are
Radiating confidence, like a shining star
With each word, we speak our voices gleam
Empowered queens, majestic in our dreams

Our superpower lies in knowing our true selves
Unveiling strength from within, where greatness dwells
But our Girl Power blooms when we uplift each other
Supporting, and encouraging, sisters lifting one another

No battle for attention, that's not our style
We choose to uplift, going the extra mile
No tearing down, no gossip, no strife
Instead, celebrating, enriching each other's life

Deep within our souls, our work remains secure
Confident and strong, our spirits ever pure
No need for comparison or demeaning words
Unity and empowerment are the chords that surge

Supporting one another, forging bonds so strong
Guiding with wisdom, cheering each other along
Jealousy and envy find no place in our hearts
Only genuine care, a love that never departs

Hey, we girls know our power, our strength untamed
Standing firm in our beliefs, going unrestrained
No competition or attempts to bring one down
For we're united, wearing crowns, conquering the crown

Embracing our uniqueness, each one a radiant light
Valuing differences, like stars in the night
With hearts filled with love, we illuminate the way
Knowing our worth, the power in all we do and say

No spreading rumors or malicious lies
No gossip's poison or deceit that defies
No rolling eyes, no diminishing another's shine
Instead, we lift each other, unity our lifeline

In this journey of Girl Power, we'll forever rise
Lifting one another higher, as we courageously thrive
Bound together, we create a world that's inspired
Empowering, embracing, and forever aspiring

Girl, when you truly know and embrace your superpower,
the magic it holds is simply extraordinary.

Shake Off The Doubt

Shake off the doubt, let it scatter to the wind
Embrace your strength within, and allow it to ascend
Though uncertainty may burden you, you possess the key
Banish ambiguity, unleash your dreams to be

Release the residue clinging to your thoughts
Unleash the worries that have tied you in knots
With each step forward, leave doubt behind
And let the dust settle deep within your mind

Your shoes carry dreams, so dust them off with care
Walk with conviction, where possibility gleams fair
Let the ground beneath you be a canvas of hope
As you journey onward, with a resolute scope

Doubt attempts to silence, clutching with might
Through fresh eyes, reclaim your inner light
Brush away fear, watch it crumble and fade
Forge ahead, undeterred, let courage be displayed

With every stride, leave doubt behind
Let intention be the wind, propelling your mind
In the settling dust, a new chapter takes flight
Where resilience triumphs, doubt dissolves in sight

For in the dust lies the remnants of the past
The worries and fears that won't forever last
Shake them off, with each confident stride
And let your true essence, unfettered, abide

Shake off the voices that question your worth
You are competent, genuine, filled with mirth
The doubts of others will try but in vain
Your path is divine come sunshine or rain

Though hesitation may linger, it has no control
Over the fire within that ignites your soul
Don't let it cloud your vision or dim your light
Believe in yourself, and soar to magnificent heights

With newfound clarity, your path shall unfold
As you leave doubt behind, and embrace the bold
Shake off the doubt, let your spirit arise
And watch as your dreams soar beyond the skies

So brush off the shadows that dim your light
Let determination guide you, through the darkest night
With every step taken, with courage anew
Shake off the doubt, and let your spirit breakthrough

Your shoes carry dreams, so dust them off with
care and walk like you know they're there.

Take The Stage

Own the stage, let your energy surge
Dance to the rhythm of your own tune
Within your heart, you'll find the flow
Step by step, let your true self glow

Onto the stage, none shall block your view
In your splendor, may your light break through
Under the spotlight reveal your destined place
Let aspirations thrive, the uncertainty you erase

Center stage, let your phenomenon unfurl
With each step, enchant the watching world
Just as God gave gifts to each of them
No one can take away your unique gem

Amidst the crowd's gaze, remain true
No need to upstage or steal what's not due
Inspire and uplift, like a melodious tune
Stay grounded in authenticity, your boon

Yearn for more within the glowin' lights' allure
But let not ego or pride be what you adore
Leap with grace, as if you're gracefully flying
A spirit soaring like a beautiful bird defying

With kindness and compassion, keep evolving
Through graceful movements, a story resolve
Success lies not in stealing the show
But in touching hearts, inspiring others to sow

Embrace challenges, overcome each test
Perseverance guides you to your best
Through triumph and failure, stay the course
Drawing strength from within, own your force

So dance, dear soul with all your might
Let your words and movements take flight
On life's grand stage, let your spirit thrive
Like a Broadway musical truly alive

No one can upstage your glow; if they move wrong it shines brighter.

Eternal Grace

Inside my book, heartfelt notes reside
Penned with tender ink, love's gentle guide
If my words can inspire someone's dream
To love beyond oneself, like a sparkling gleam

If my words can inspire someone's soul
Embrace love's essence, make them whole
If I can bring back beauty to their world
Then my living won't be in vain, unfurled

Let compassion find its place, let dreams rise
As hearts embrace kindness, a treasure in disguise
May this poem's melody resonate with your core
A tender reminder, love makes us whole and more

In this journey of hearts, we find our place
Empowered by love, enveloped in grace
May this collection inspire, hearts set aglow
Unleashing love's inspiration, an eternal overflow

"Spreading love, inspiring hearts, shining love's light bringing smiles and laughter, a magic we all share."

About The Author

Aurora L. Threats is a true gem - guided by love and grace. "A Gumbo of Poems & Quotes" is her second book, a dazzling collection that showcases her breathtaking beauty, extraordinary talent, and boundless creativity. Aurora invites you to savor her invigorating medley of verses and inspiring quotes. She has prepared a veritable feast for the senses and the soul. Get ready to be captivated by her artistry!

Within this collection, step right up and witness the grand premiere of Supercilious the poem. This magnificent poem graces the pages of "A Gumbo of Poems & Quotes!" Delve into this thought-provoking commentary that tackles the harsh truth of how some judge, label and exclude others based on factors such as wealth, privilege, and biases.

Aurora beautifully sculptured a storytelling approach to blend artistic styles and techniques together to produce the critically acclaimed short film Supercilious which was nominated by the 54th NAACP Image Awards for Best Animated Short Form (Motion Picture).

Supercilious, the award-winning film made an impression in the film festivals. Aurora's incredible creativity was honored with numerous accolades at film festivals worldwide including winning Best Animation (ARG International Film Festival) in Paris, France; named Best Kids Movie IBDF (International Black & Diversity Film Festival) in Ontario, Canada. Also, an Official Selection (TAFF The African Film Festival) in Dallas, TX, and Semi-Finalist (The Afro Animation Short Film Award) in Toronto, Canada all within the 2022 calendar year.

Aurora's animated short film demonstrates her unwavering dedication to crafting content that truly matters. She blazed a trail that ultimately led her to become the first-ever female from the United States to collaborate with Ghana, Africa on an animated short film.

Aurora resides within the vibrant metroplex of Dallas/Ft. Worth, TX. Yet she still cherishes the fond memories of Lake Providence where she was born and raised within the picturesque landscape of the Louisiana Delta. Aurora is a proud graduate of Grambling State University where she earned a B.S. in Speech & Theatre Education. Taking the university's motto to heart, "Where Everybody is Somebody," Aurora has made sure to practice and apply these powerfully profound words to every aspect of her life, which shows in all she does. Additionally, she holds an M.S. in Human Relations & Bus. from Amberton University in Garland, TX.

We encourage you to sit back and enjoy every page of Aurora's "A Gumbo of Poems & Quotes." With each turn, you will be uplifted and inspired by the beauty of her words, the warmth of her spirit, and the depth of her wisdom. Allow yourself to be carried away by the rhythm of her verse and the power of her message.

Aurora's work is a true gift to us all. We have no doubt that it will continue to touch and transform hearts for generations to come.

Printed in the United States
by Baker & Taylor Publisher Services